ELECTRICIAN

Published in the United States of America by Cherry Lake Publishing
Ann Arbor, Michigan
www.cherrylakepublishing.com

Content Adviser: Matt Whybark, Vedder Electric, Ann Arbor, Michigan
Reading Adviser: Marla Conn MS, Ed., Literacy specialist, Read-Ability, Inc.

Photo Credits: © Phovoir/Shutterstock, cover, 1, 11; © Jupiterimages/Thinkstock, 5; © Everett Historical/Shutterstock, 6; © Polonez/Shutterstock, 8; © Alexander Gatsenko/istock, 9; © goodluz/Shutterstock, 10; © Constantine Androsoff/Shutterstock, 13; © CHAINFOTO24/Shutterstock, 14; © John Kroetch/istock, 16; © Lisa F. Young/istock, 19; © NathanMarx/istock, 20; © Monkey Business Images/Shutterstock, 22; © SolStock/istock, 25; © Praphan Jampala/Shutterstock, 26; © Gary Whitton/Shutterstock, 28

Library of Congress Cataloging-in-Publication Data
Names: Labrecque, Ellen, author.
Title: Electrician / Ellen Labrecque.
Description: Ann Arbor, Michigan : Cherry Lake Publishing, [2016] |
Series: Cool vocational careers | Audience: Grades 4-6. | Includes bibliographical
    references and index.
Identifiers: LCCN 2015046146| ISBN 9781634710626 (hardcover) |
    ISBN 9781634712606 (pbk.) | ISBN 9781634711616 (pdf) | ISBN 9781634713597 (ebook)
Subjects: LCSH: Electricians—Juvenile literature. | Electrical engineering—
Vocational guidance—Juvenile literature.
Classification: LCC TK159 .L33 2016 | DDC 621.319/24/023—dc23
LC record available at http://lccn.loc.gov/2015046146

Cherry Lake Publishing would like to acknowledge the work of the Partnership for 21st Century Learning.
Please visit *www.p21.org* for more information.

Printed in the United States of America
Corporate Graphics

ABOUT THE AUTHOR

Ellen Labrecque is a freelance writer living in Yardley, Pennsylvania. Previously, she was a senior editor at *Sports Illustrated Kids*. Ellen loves to travel and then learn about new places and people she can write about in her books.

TABLE OF CONTENTS

CHAPTER 1

Light It Up!

Imagine a world of darkness, a place where light comes only from fire and the sun. What kind of world would that be? Actually, it's the world that people lived in for most of human history. It's the world before humans discovered electricity.

Electricity has only been used during the past 100 to 150 years. Yet think of how important it has become in that time. We would not be able to light our homes and businesses without it. We need it to power the electronics we use every day. Computers, TVs, and air conditioners run on electricity. So do machines in hospitals. Don't forget about equipment in factories. You can probably think of many more things that would not work without electricity.

Most people use electrical devices every day.

Benjamin Franklin experimented with electricity.

In June 1752, Benjamin Franklin flew a kite during a lightning storm. He hung a metal key from the kite's string. Electricity traveled down the string when the kite was struck by lightning. This caused the key to spark. Franklin discovered that lightning was caused by electricity. He also realized that electricity could travel along power lines.

One hundred years passed before scientists discovered how to turn electricity into light. Many scientists around the world helped with the invention of the lightbulb. They included Joseph Swan in England and Thomas Edison in the United States.

Edison's idea for the lightbulb was part of a larger plan. He invented a system that would create electricity. It would also deliver it to homes and businesses. People began using this system in the late 1880s.

Since then, electricians have had the job of setting up that system. They must also maintain it. Electricity travels along a path from where it is produced to where it is used. Electricians make sure the electricity moves safely at each step along that path. Some electricians work at the power plants where electricity is produced. Others work on power lines. These lines carry

21st Century Content

People spend a lot of their day plugging in things to get electricity. They plug in their lamps. They plug in their phones. But, in the near future, electricity could run without plugging in anything at all. Just as we now have wireless Internet, we will all have wireless electricity someday. Do you want to find out more about it? Visit www.witricity.com to learn all about the wireless future.

Thunderstorms can cause power outages.

electricity from power plants to homes and businesses. Some
electricians work on the wires, outlets, and switches inside
buildings.

Houses often lose electricity when power lines are knocked
down during big storms. Electricians hurry to the scene. They fix
the power lines and bring power back to buildings left in the dark.
These electricians must often work outside during storms. They
face the elements, such as wind, rain, and snow. They work under
dangerous conditions. Electricity and water are a deadly mix!

Sometimes electricians need to repair damaged power lines.

Blueprints can help electricians understand how a building's wiring is set up.

Homes and businesses rely on electricians to keep things running smoothly.

Electricians install wires and panels in new buildings. They read **blueprints** to see where everything goes. Electricians are also called in to repair wiring in older buildings. Old wiring can cause fires. Electricians may replace the panels, wiring, and outlets in these older buildings. This makes the electrical system work more effectively and safely. As keepers of the power system, electricians have many jobs!

On the Job

It all begins at the power plant. Big machines called **generators** change forms of energy into electricity. The energy might come from burning fuels. These include coal, oil, or gas. These fuels produce harmful waste that is released into the air.

There are also cleaner ways to generate the energy needed to create electricity. **Hydropower** uses the force of rushing water to power the generators. Wind power uses the force of wind. Solar power comes from sunlight.

There are three big categories of electricians in the United States. The first category is commercial and industrial electricians. These are the ones who take care of the equipment at the power plants. They make sure the power keeps moving. They also make sure that big heating and air-conditioning systems and

Hydroelectric power plants store electricity for later use.

manufacturing machinery all stay working. These electricians connect large cables from generators to **transformers**. Transformers can increase or decrease the **voltage** of electricity. Voltage is the force that pushes electricity through electric power lines.

Transformers at power plants are called step-up transformers. They increase voltage. This allows the electricity to travel longer distances while using less energy. This electricity is dangerous and not ready for people to use.

The electricity travels out of the power plant through power

Electricians wear special gear for protection.

lines. Some power lines run under the ground. Others run above the ground. They are attached to large metal towers and wooden or concrete utility poles.

The second big category of electricians is called residential electricians. These are the electricians who keep the power going in your homes and apartment buildings. They may work in new homes by installing new wiring. Or they may focus on maintaining, remodeling, and fixing current houses and apartment buildings.

The third big category of electricians is called lineworkers.

They are the ones responsible for bringing electricity from power generation plants to all the buildings where the other electricians work. They install and maintain all the power lines you see around your town or city. This can be really dangerous! They work around larger towers in all kinds of weather, and they work with really high voltage electricity! Lineworkers use special equipment and clothing to help them stay safe.

One tool they use is a truck that has a bucket on the back. The bucket is big enough for a lineworker to stand in. A long

21st Century Content

As of 2015, only 18 percent of all power lines are underground in the United States. But when storms hit, winds, broken tree limbs, ice, and snow all knock power lines down. This causes electricity to go out. So why don't electric companies bury power lines under the ground where they'll be protected? First, that kind of undertaking would require billions and billions of dollars. And even though buried lines are protected from wind, ice, and tree damage, they could still be damaged by flooding. In addition, if the underground power lines do fail, they are a lot harder to fix!

Electricians sometimes go up in buckets to reach the lines.

arm raises the bucket. That way, the worker can reach the tops of utility poles and towers. The bucket is made of **insulated** material. This means the material does not allow electricity to pass through it. The bucket keeps the worker safe from powerful electricity. Lineworkers also protect themselves by wearing special gloves and boots. Of all electricians, lineworkers have the most dangerous job. They must repair power lines no matter the situation. This often means working in the dark. Rain, snow, and high winds can't stop a lineworker either. The power must be restored. The lights must go on!

CHAPTER 3

Becoming an Electrician

What does it take to become an electrician? Electricians need clear and focused minds. They must pay careful attention to their work. Otherwise, they can put themselves and others in danger. Service electricians and technicians need good problem-solving skills. They need to be able to learn how to use specialized tools. Other electricians who work in construction need to lift heavy items. How heavy? They might have to lift more than 50 pounds (23 kilograms). They also have to be able to use tools to bend metal **conduit** pipes.

Stamina is also important. Electricians may need to climb up tall poles. They may have to stay balanced there for a long time during bad weather. They might also have to stand or kneel for hours. At the same time, they must stay focused on the tiniest

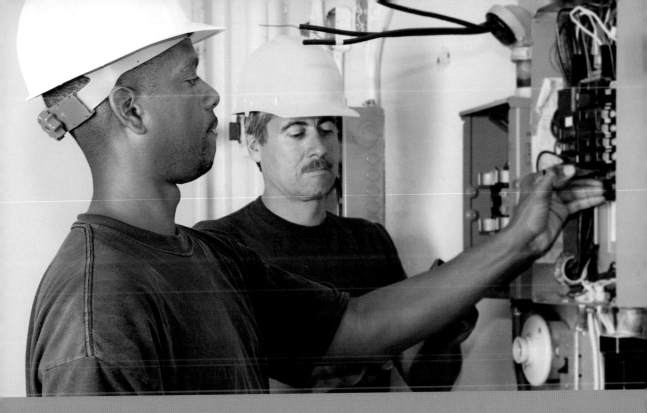

Electricians who are just starting out are called apprentices.

details of their work.

Electricians need to be at least 18 years old. In high school, a future electrician should take lots of math classes, as well as physics and engineering. Most electricians start out as **apprentices**. They learn skills from experienced electricians. Apprentices work during the day. They get paid while learning the job. At night, they take classes to learn things like how to read blueprints and the rules of safe wiring. They also take classes in math, electronics, and job safety. People who want to be apprentices need to pass a test that measures math, reading, and

A good electrician can find solutions to difficult problems.

fine motor skills. People who pass the test have to wait for an apprenticeship to open up. This could take several months.

Apprentices begin with simple tasks. These include drilling holes or attaching conduit pipes to the wall. The apprentice will observe the whole construction process while learning and asking questions. As the apprentice gains skills, he or she will move on to more complex tasks. Apprentices train on the job for 3 to 5 years. Many electricians keep taking classes after they finish their apprenticeships. They learn about telephones, computers, and other topics.

After an apprenticeship, an electrician's next step is to take a licensing exam. A license proves that the electrician has worked hard and put in years of study and training. Electricians continue learning and training even after getting licensed. They need to keep up with new **technology**. They also learn about changes in the field.

Paul Fiore is an electrician in New Jersey. Paul started his career as an apprentice with the International Brotherhood of Electrical Workers Local 102. He worked as an apprentice for five years. Then he became a journeyman and kept moving his way

Some high schools offer courses that teach basic electrical skills.

up from there. He worked on commercial buildings, including powerhouses, refineries, and paper mills. Today, Paul is the assistant director of his union, where he helps select and train the new apprentices.

Paul suggests taking some basic electrical courses in high school to get a start on becoming an electrician. "That shows you have an interest in the field," he explains.

Paul also says there is a lot of competition to get a spot as an apprentice. "Last year we had 400 applicants," he says about his union. "And we could only accept 50." He says that apprentices aren't expected to have much background knowledge. "But they must be really interested in learning while on the job. Being an electrician is a really intellectual job."

Paul explains that electricians are constantly taking continuing education classes to stay updated on new techniques and technology. "It's a changing industry," he says. "You have to stay updated on the new laws and rules."

Life and Career Skills

Here are an experienced electrician's top tips for becoming an electrician.

1. *Take a lot of math courses in high school, especially algebra. "We use math in our job all the time," explains licensed electrician Paul Fiore.*
2. *Play team sports. "In this job, we need guys who are team players," Paul says.*
3. *Take safety guidelines seriously. "Being an electrician can be dangerous. You must be prepared."*

CHAPTER 4

The Future Is Bright

Job opportunities for electricians are growing rapidly, and the field is expected to grow well into the future. Every new building constructed requires extensive electrical wiring, and many older homes and buildings need to be updated. Also, electric companies are building more and more power plants. This will create new jobs for electricians. The demand for highly skilled electricians will also increase as new technology appears. Buildings of the future will need wiring for more advanced control systems and computers.

The same will be true for more advanced communications equipment. Electricians with knowledge of voice, data, and video electronics will be in greater demand. Factories continue to add robots and advanced manufacturing systems. These will require the setup and maintenance of detailed wiring systems.

As more houses are built, more electricians are needed.

Electricity is necessary in the field of manufacturing.

The nation's **infrastructure** always needs to be maintained and upgraded to meet new safety codes. Utility poles, power lines, and other parts need to be fixed or replaced as they age. Lighting and heating systems continue to become more advanced. Modern buildings often have computers that control lighting and heating. The electricians of the future will need to know how to work on these systems.

The search for clean energy continues. Experts try to provide electricity for more people without damaging the environment. Advances in wind and solar power will become more important. Electricians will have to be trained in these areas as they develop.

21st Century Content

The United States Department of Labor estimates that employment opportunities for electricians will increase by about 14 percent between 2014 and 2024. They will add 85,900 jobs for a total of 714,700 positions. The average salary for an electrician is $51,110 a year. The most sought-after electricians will be the ones who have the widest variety of skills.

Why do you think electricians continue to be in demand? Do you think people will always need their services?

Solar panels, which convert the sun's energy to usable electricity, are becoming more popular.

Matt Day loves his job as an electrician. He loves working outside and in different locations every day. "I'm not an office person," he says. "While others are wondering what's it like outside, I know what it's like because I'm in it." There are downsides, though. Getting shocked can be scary, but it always reminds him to find the power source before he starts working. "We have no extra lives in the game of life," he says.

Being an electrician will only require more skills in the future. Matt is seeing more advanced electrical setups. Smart houses are one example. In a smart house, the electrical systems are linked to a computer system. Some of these systems are controlled over the Internet.

Wind and solar power are promising sources of energy. But our electrical infrastructure will have to be remade to make the most of these. The electricians of the future will be doing that work.

Picture a normal day in your life. Now imagine that same day without electricity. How would it be different? By now, you probably realize that electricity plays an important role in many parts of our lives. Products that use electricity help us in many ways. They allow us to see in the dark. They allow us to heat our homes. Electricity also powers the machines that entertain us. Someone will always be needed to create and maintain power systems. Will that someone be you?

Think About It

Ask your parent or teacher if they have ever tried to fix the electricity in their house. Is this a safe thing to do without training? Why or why not?

When you slide down a slide, does your hair ever stand on end? Have you ever received a shock after walking across a rug and touching something else? This is caused by static electricity! Have you ever heard this term? Do you know what causes it?

Do you think it is important to continue to take classes and learn new things as an electrician? Why or why not?

For More Information

BOOKS

Dawson, Patricia. *An Electrician's Job*. New York: Cavendish Square Publishing, 2015.

Graham, Ian. *You Wouldn't Want to Live Without Electricity*! New York: Franklin Watts, 2015.

Parker, Steve. *Electricity*. London: DK Publishing, 2013.

WEB SITES

BBC—Shock and Awe: The Story of Electricity
www.bbc.co.uk/programmes/p00kjq6d
Watch videos about the invention of electricity.

Bureau of Labor Statistics—Occupational Outlook Handbook: Electricians
www.bls.gov/ooh/construction-and-extraction/electricians.htm
Learn more about what electricians do.

How Stuff Works—How Electricity Works
http://science.howstuffworks.com/electricity.htm
Read more about what electricity is, where it comes from, and how humans use it.

GLOSSARY

apprentices (uh-PREN-tis-iz) people who learn a trade by working with an expert

blueprints (BLOO-prints) drawings or plans for a project

conduit (KON-doo-it) pipe that protects electric wires

fine motor skills (FINE MOH-tur SKILLZ) the ability to complete small detailed tasks, usually with your hands

generators (JEN-uh-ray-turz) machines that produce electricity

hydropower (HYE-droh-pou-ur) electricity created by the movement of water

infrastructure (IN-fruh-struk-chur) the basic framework of a system

insulated (IN-suh-lay-tid) treated in a special way to keep electricity from passing through

stamina (STAM-uh-nuh) the ability to continue doing something for a long period of time

technology (tek-NAH-luh-jee) the use of science and engineering to do practical things, such as making businesses more efficient

transformers (tranz-FORM-urz) devices that raise or lower the force of electricity

voltage (VOHL-tij) a measure of the force of electricity

INDEX